Hanging By A Thread
The Plight Of The Alabama Beach Mouse

By Myrt Jones

TABLE OF CONTENTS

APPRECIATION

I personally wish to thank these individuals as they helped in so many ways:

This started life as a children's book. Lynda Crane, a local librarian did a reading, assured me this in no way resembled a children's book, so I took another path.

Stephanie Jones, my youngest daughter patiently read, reread, edited, reedited, supported my numerous efforts in writing this book during those many months yet continued to believe in it.

Sharon Jones, my oldest daughter and graduate of the Ringling School of Art provided the mouse illustrations used throughout the book, injecting amusing relief, plus the neat title for the book.

Deborah Yurt, Chris Stanford, Kristine Polizzi, Emily Ensore-Gibson, Michael Campbell and the very friendly, professional staff who protect and oversee the Audubon Society's environmental documents that provided much needed information for this book in the University of South Alabama's McCall Rare Book and Manuscript Library.

Jo Billups read a first draft and became hugely supportive. She and Karen Harvill play their guitars before groups while singing songs about environmental issues in travels around the country.

Hank Caddell, an eco-warrior and local lawyer protected the beach mouse all of these years in coastal Alabama and acquires properties for the Bon Secour NWR. Hank edited and made suggestions for the book.

Skipper Tonsmiere, past member of the Mobile Bay Audubon Society and coastal developer provided additional history about his involvement in saving and acquiring coastal lands, particularly the Perdue Tract

William Lynn, Certified Wildlife Biologist with U.S. Fish & Wildlife Service in Daphne edited, provided photos and other material.

Dave Morine, Representative with The Nature Conservancy was instrumental in acquiring the first three parcels of the BSNWR.

Don W. Linzey, a mammologist was instrumental in organizing the first MBAS and helped edit the book.

Renewed a blast from the past when Alicia Linzey Hulse, a friend, mammologist and organizer of the first MBAS supplied useful information for the book.

Last but certainly not least is Martin Smith, my young computer 'whiz' who keeps my computer running, then when given a pile of papers places all of the pieces in the right spots, turning it into another fantastic book on Amazon for the reader to enjoy.

If I have forgotten anyone, please forgive me. Many thanks to the beach mouse as it has truly been MY coastal hero/heroine all of these years!

ABBREVIATIONS

Alabama Beach Mouse
    ABM

Alabama Coastal Heritage Trust Fund
    ACHTF

Alabama Department of Conservation & Natural Resources
    ADCNR

Alabama Department of Economic Development
    ADO

Alabama Department of Environmental Management
    ADEM

Alabama State Port Authority
    ASPA

Beach Mouse
    BM

Bon Secour National Wildlife Refuge
    BSNWR

British Petroleum
    BP

Chamber of Commerce
    COC

Clean Air Act
    CAA

Clean Water Act
CWA

Coastal Area Board
CAB

Coastal Construction Line
CCL

Coastal Zone Management Act
CZMA

Corps of Engineers
COE

Department of Interior
DOI

Endangered Species Act
ESA

Environmental Impact Statement
EIS

European Union
EU

Federal Emergency Management Act
FEMA

Federal Flood Insurance Program
FFIP

Findings of No Significant Impact
FONSI

Gulf Environmental Benefit Fund
> GEBF

Gulf of Mexico
> GOM

Gulf State Park
> GSP

Habitat Conservation Plan
> HCP

Incidental Takings Permit
> ITP

International Union for Conservation of Nature
> IUCN

Invasive Alien Species
> IAS

Little Dauphin Island
> LDI

Mobile Bay Audubon Society
> MBAS

National Environmental Policy Act
> NEPA

National Fish & Wildlife Foundation
> NFWF

National Marine Fisheries Services
> NMFS

Little Point Clear
    LPC

The Nature Conservancy
    TNC

The Conservation Fund
    TCF

United States Fish & Wildlife Service
    USFWS

United States Environmental Protection Agency
    EPA

THE ALABAMA BEACH MOUSE

Since the days of Mickey Mouse and Ratatouille there hasn't been a more appealing rodent than the Alabama Beach Mouse (ABM). Unfortunately, because of our single-minded destruction of their habitat, this little mouse has become an endangered species, living on borrowed time, on a tiny stretch of Alabama coastline. We've shrunk their home range and reduced their numbers to such an alarming extent that extinction is a real possibility and once the Beach Mouse (BM) is gone, it's gone forever!

ALABAMA GULF COAST: FORT MORGAN PENINSULA

The only place on earth you can still find the Alabama Beach Mouse is along a mere fourteen mile stretch of fragile coastal barrier lands in Baldwin County, Alabama. The area extends from the west end of the Fort Morgan Peninsula eastward to the Perdido Bay Inlet and Ono Island.

It was recently discovered that the BM also depends on the elevated scrub sand and transition dune systems found further inland on the north side of the island, closer to Mobile Bay. These elevated dune systems provide safer neighborhoods, additional habitat, plus a variety of foods for all of the creatures during and following storms. Protecting these areas from development is crucial if the BM and other threatened and endangered species living in this coastal area are to survive.

OLD FIELD MOUSE

The BM comprises the eight subspecies of the old field mouse (Peromyscus polionotus). These mammals are usually found throughout the dry, sandy habitats on barrier islands, keys or coastal peninsulas in N.E. Mississippi; Baldwin County, Alabama; Georgia; South Carolina; and Florida. The five Gulf Coast subspecies of old field mouse distributed in Alabama and Florida are the St. Andrews Beach Mouse, Perdido Key Beach Mouse, Choctawatchee Beach Mouse, Alabama Beach Mouse and Santa Rosa Beach Mouse.

The three other species are the Pallid Beach Mouse, found in two locations in Florida, and they are constantly being threatened. The Southeastern Beach Mouse and the Anastasia Island Beach Mouse found on Florida's Atlantic coast face the same problems as the Alabama and Perdido Key Beach Mouse.

An article titled Small Matters found in The Voice of Defenders of Wildlife (Becca Bryan, winter 2019) asks: "What weighs no more than five pennies, is only five-and-a-half inches long and can save eroding sand dunes in Florida: The Perdido Key beach mouse." This tiny, federally endangered creature, struggles to survive in the face of continued habitat loss from land development and cat predation.

Fortunately, people are working together to boost the gene pool in the wild and protect more habitats. This helps the mouse and also benefits us by protecting the dunes that help contain storm surge.

SURVIVAL OF THE BEACH MOUSE?

In 1979, two exceptional men became concerned about the survival of the five subspecies of BM living in the dune systems on Florida and Alabama's gulf coast. They knew that our healthy dune systems existed because the BM provided numerous benefits, not only for nature, but for mankind.

Dr. Stephen Humphrey of Florida State Museum in Tallahassee joined forces and signed a petition with Dr. Dan Holliman, a biology professor at Birmingham Southern College. They requested the Department of Interior (DOI), specifically the United States Fish & Wildlife Service (USFWS) to review the status of Florida's Choctawhatchee Beach Mouse, Alabama's Perdido Key Beach Mouse and Alabama's Beach Mouse (ABM), for possible inclusion to the Endangered Species List. The Endangered Species Act (ESA) was the only legal process available that could save the mouse.

Dr. Holliman had conducted studies on the ABM (Peromyscus polionotus ammobates) and noted in his petition:

"There does appear to be some threat to their continual survival, as the beach and dunes on which the mice depend are being lost to increased development pressures and the mice were becoming more vulnerable. It was imperative their habitat be protected as an endangered species, as he estimated the mouse population to be less than 500 surviving."

His research helped usher in their protection and once the BM was added to the Endangered List it assured that:

1) All federal agencies guarantee that no actions authorized with federal funding could jeopardize the mice or destroy their habitat, or otherwise consult with the USFWS prior to final decision

2) No person would be allowed to trap, kill, harass, take or pursue mice without a permit. Permits would be issued only for any action which would be beneficial to the mice, such as a study or recovery project. These would be done by knowledgeable persons with a recovery plan that would ensure survival and eventual recovery of the animal.

These extra precautions also provided a bulwark against loss of our coastal resources to unchecked development and prevented extinction of not only several species of BM, but other threatened and endangered species in the areas as well.

When the DOI published their decision to *consider* adding the BM as candidates to the list in the Federal Registry, a Public Hearing was held in Gulf Shores on August 28, 1984. This provided an opportunity for over 200 citizens to have input. As President of the Mobile Bay Audubon Society (MBAS) I joined forces with others and strongly supported the addition of all three of the BM species to the Endangered Species List.

WHY ALL THE FUSS?

At the meeting Dr. Steve Carey, a Mobile biologist made these valid points about the value of *things:*

 "Why all the fuss over a little mouse and just how much was the wildlife worth in coastal Alabama?...it's relatively easy to assign a monetary value to commercially important animals such as blue crabs, shrimp, speckled trout and white-tailed deer, but what about species that don't have an actual monetary value like the Alabama Beach Mouse? They have no direct economic value, but after all how much is a bluebird's song worth to you? A price cannot be assigned for aesthetics or ecological value, as they have no economic benefits unless you consider the invaluable services they provide for Mankind. The mice are not trapped for food or clothing, but are cute, provided you ever get the chance to see one.

Their contributions are invaluable, because they do stuff that most of you aren't even aware of as the mice are very fond of sea oat seeds which they collect and bury in a chamber of their burrows, to eat at a later date. Many are never recovered and sprout, growing up through the dune system and become mature sea oats plants that help stabilize the dune systems. The dunes provide natural buffers between the sea and inland areas and help protect the developed areas on the Gulf Coast.

Each species is really a priceless commodity. Once extinct it can never be replaced at any price, yet we continue to develop our beautiful Gulf Coast, but let us remember that the loss of a species is a very high price to pay for short-term gains."

OPPOSTION GETS INVOLVED

The Mobile Chamber of Commerce, Politicians and Developers were the groups who resisted the idea of more regulations. They claimed protection of the ABM would adversely affect property values on the Alabama coast. I'm always surprised by this reasoning since their desire to be unregulated would allow for an unchecked greed-driven destruction of the things which make our gulf coast such an attractive area to live in.

The Mobile Press Register, a biased pro- business newspaper represented their side, and ran an article making it clear exactly where they stood on environmental issues, along the gulf coast. *"Rats! Another roadblock seen for condominiums, little brown mice threatening to grind the wheels of multi-million dollar condo developments to a screeching or squeaking halt."* They always *made it clear where they stood on environmental issues along the gulf coast.*

Alabama has always suffered from a lack of gifted political leadership. The Politicians we do have always seem to bear watching as an inordinate number of them tend to land in jail.

This book shows how the involvement of a few concerned citizens resulted in some of the more positive outcomes in the area, especially on the environmental front. So, if you are someone who enjoys seeing large undeveloped stretches of pristine coastal land saved in perpetuity then read on to discover how that happened on the Alabama's gulf coast. Trust me; it wasn't because an Alabama politician saw the value of it first.

MOST ENDANGERED

In July 0f 1985, the USFWS identified the ABM as one of the most endangered mammals in North America and believed it was headed for Extinction. They decided to add the mouse to the Endangered Species List as being of Highest Conservation Concern and published their decision in the Federal Register.

MOUSE HABITAT

The BM lives within the beach/ dune system and depend upon a maze of sandy, vegetated corridors for traveling from one place to another. They travel on these small sandy vegetated covered paths called ingress… egress corridors to forage for food and water, collect construction material for their dens, visit neighbors, raise little mice and outpace many predators. These corridors provide much needed safety and protection, which the mouse desperately needs, while it goes about its numerous duties.

The mice construct 'unique underground engineered burrows'
at the base and sides of dunes, other sandy vegetated areas
and in the shallow, depressed swale areas found between the
dune systems. These swale areas provide numerous benefits
for the mice and other creatures such as transportation
corridors, watering holes, shelter and feeding areas. They
contain salt grass, yaupon, black needle rush, various berry
plants, sedges and rushes, items the mice use for food,
construction of their burrows, and as bedding for their nests.

Burrows have three compartments and provide safe places for
the mice. One is used for sleeping, eating, raising families and
procreating; while another provides storage for a variety of
foods; then there is a sandy trap door at the end of each tunnel
that the mouse can easily pop out, offering an escape hatch, in
case of predators.

COASTAL HERO

To my mind, the ABM is a genuine coastal hero. This brave
little survivor doesn't know that its very existence, as an
endangered species, ensures that greedy developers can't
destroy every inch of our natural Gulf coastline. Isn't it great a
tiny mouse has that kind of power?

SYMBIOTIC RELATIONSHIP: BENEFITS AND VALUES

The many symbiotic relationships within our dune systems provide invaluable benefits for mankind and nature. These beautiful natural sandy areas continually rebuild themselves by collecting, recycling and depositing sand particles constantly found within the surrounding environment. They:

- Provide sea oats and other foods for numerous birds, marsh rabbits and beach mice.
- Are protected as the Alabama Legislature enacted a law in 1973 prohibiting walking on the dunes and picking sea oats.
- Provide insects in the beach sands and bushes for birds, crabs, mammals, etc.
- Act as buffers, absorbing and lessening the catastrophic impacts from waves, surges, torrential rains, high tides, floodwaters, salty sprays and violent winds, associated with our frequent destructive tropical storms and hurricanes.
- They also protect manmade structures and human lives.
- Provide a mix of vegetation which can be used for shelter, safety, food, building supplies and sleeping pads for the mouse and other wildlife.
- These coastal dune areas are so valuable that beneficial boardwalks are constructed over them to minimize human impacts, while allowing public access to the beach and Gulf waters.
- These areas provide scientific opportunities as well as aesthetics.

People need to realize there are other threats than just the destructive projects of man. Global climatic changes from greenhouse gases are causing a rising sea level, which also places coastal systems and any man-made structures in peril. Creatures will be placed in jeopardy, and once they're gone they are gone forever.

MONETIZE ECOLOGICAL VALUES

One way to protect the numerous benefits of these natural areas is to *monetize them* to help counter the bloated economic figures used by the Chamber of Commerce, politicians and developers in promoting their destructive projects.

The first person to assign `dollar' values for natural systems was Dr. Eugene Odum, who helped inspire the environmental movement in the seventies, and is the Father of Modern Ecology. He joined forces with Dr. James Gosselink and Dr. R. Pope of LSU, as others had trouble placing money value on the `free works' of nature.

Dr. Odum assigned the first dollar value of $83,000/acre on Georgia's priceless coastal wetlands. He realized they provide numerous benefits for Mother Nature and Mankind, such as nursery areas for commercial and recreational fisheries. These natural areas disperse and hold floodwaters; provide variety of food sources and habitats for marine life, variety of birds, mammals and raptors; are potential areas for aqua cultural development for shellfish and they provide fantastic tertiary waste assimilation processes. His figures proved to be high powered ammunition for environmentalists, as it was the first time natural areas and processes were given a tangible dollar value.

The assigned value of $83,000.00 was used to save prime coastal wetlands in Mobile Harbor from the Corps of Engineers and Alabama State Port Authority's proposed destructive, dredge and fill projects. For details read my book, "Chronicle of An Eco-Warrior: Relating South Alabama's Environmental Issues." It's available on Amazon.

SCRUB TRANSITION ZONES

In 1983, Dr. Dan Holliman wondered just how the mice could survive storms and suggested that they might be found in a third coastal habitat: the scrub/transition zone. These areas are further landward of the primary and secondary dunes systems and closer to Mobile Bay. Dr. Holliman believed that the scrub habitat values might serve as a refugium, during and after severe environmental events and suggested more studies be done in order to better understand, identify and appreciate these systems.

During numerous coastal surveys undertaken in 1997, scientists discovered the mice had used their natural warning systems and determined that Hurricane Danny was headed their way. They gathered up friends and family and headed north on white sandy evacuation corridors, crossed the highway, finally reaching the safety of their elevated scrub/transition `hurricane shelters.'

VARIETY OF ELEVATED SYSTEMS

These elevated systems are characterized as containing:

- Dwarfed live oak trees (Quercus geminate) and Scrubby oak systems (Quercus virginiana) are small, scrubby thickets with thick green leaves and surrounded or bases covered with sand. The ABM love to gather and store the small dark green edible acorns in their burrows.

- Small palm tree (Serenoa repens) berries are edible, and have a strong oily blue cheese and intense peppery blast taste, which may be used for medicinal purpose.
- There are the Sandhill-rosemary shrubs (Ceratibla ericoides) that have adapted in the white sandy soils and grow from 2 to 8 feet tall, providing much needed safety.
- The sand pine (Pinus clausa) is a shrubby evergreen conifer that varies in height from 16-30' and provide seeds and safety
- The dwarfed magnolia (Magnolia grandiflora) has dense full foliage and range from 6-10.' They have a wide root system that tolerates some flooding, provides stability and bright red coated edible seeds

These special places are invaluable for keeping the mouse and other creatures safe during storms and they provide numerous benefits for Mankind as well!

CRITICAL HABITAT

In 1985, the critical habitat of the Beach Mouse was designated as 500 ft. above mean high tide line. This demarcation included Alabama's primary and secondary dunes, but excluded the scrub/transition habitats.

In February of 1999, Eric Huber with the Earth Justice Legal Defense Fund submitted a petition to the USFWS in Daphne, Alabama on behalf of the Sierra Club and the Biodiversity Legal Foundation. The critical habitat designation for the three endangered species: ABM, Perdido Key BM and Choctawhatchee BM needed to be revised. The petition indicated that the elevated systems, further from the ocean and closer to the bay were more important than previously thought.

On September 12, 2000, the USFWS released their notice in the Federal Register regarding Designation of Critical Habitat for the ABM. After an extensive process that involved public participation, it was determined there was a need for revision and added scrub dune/ vegetated transition systems, as critical habitat for the mouse.

COASTAL CONSTRUCTION LINE: CCL

In the 1980's, Hank Caddell, a Mobile attorney and Director of the Save Our Dunes Organization, sued to bring about adoption of the Coastal Construction Line (CCL) along the Gulf beaches in Mobile and Baldwin Counties. This was to defend the natural dune systems from developmental threats and protect their role as vital habitat for species and also as coastal buffers. The setback is now thirty years out of date, as the western end of Dauphin Island dune formation is 100 feet out in the Gulf of Mexico!

The cities of Gulf Shores and Orange Beach were given leave to set up their own fictitious dune lines in those days, allowing development extremely close to the water. These municipalities used bad permitting decisions, allowing development to imperil the dunes, people and threaten the ABM.

The Orange Beach municipality never seems to learn as they started the costly, never ending beach re-nourishment process to counter erosion, which truly messes up Mother Nature's natural processes.

UNRAVELING PROTECTIONS

The Officials of Perdido Key, Florida were recently granted authority by the federal government to issue permits and allow a handful of residential properties, plus a condo development in beach mouse habitat, which could affect their survival. Heaven help us and the natural world as Orange Beach and Gulf Shores may be influenced by Florida's new permitting situation allowing even more development along their coasts.

The USFWS no longer seems to have the proper funding and staff to carry out their many obligations to oversee the numerous development projects. With the environmentally hostile Trump Administration in power, people need to become involved, now more than ever to ensure endangered and threatened species, natural resources and the human element are properly protected.

Those in leadership roles of coastal planning and issuing permits need to work with Mother Nature's natural processes if the coastal areas are to remain enjoyable and healthy places for people and creatures.

DEEPWATER HORIZON BLOWOUT

The Alabama Beach Mouse population fluctuates every year from normal pressures: food availability, predation, catastrophic storms and hurricanes, but the Deepwater Horizon oil spill in the Gulf of Mexico in 2010 really brought the Mouse to the edge of extinction.

Baldwin County's beaches and vegetated dune systems in the Gulf State Park and the Bon Secour National Wildlife Refuge were heavily oiled several times. The black oil and the Corexit used to sink it, stressed and killed unknown numbers of the Alabama Beach mouse population, along with many other types of wildlife.

To make matters worse, clean-up staging areas were set up on the beaches, and numerous heavy equipment, trucks, buses and supplies passed through the dunes, allowing access to the beach. The tents and sanitary facilities were set up for the needs of hundreds of workers. Clean-up operations occurred several times and lasted for months.

BP FUNDED CLEAN-UP AND ACQUISITIONS

A lengthy federal court action followed the British Petroleum (BP) and Trans-ocean's illegal catastrophic blowout and massive oil spill in the Gulf of Mexico in 2010.

After a few years of legal bickering, billions of dollars were placed in the coffers of the Gulf Environmental Benefit Fund (GEBF) and dispersed by the National Fish & Wildlife Foundation. (NFWF) Millions of dollars were requested and dispersed to the five states bordering the Gulf of Mexico. This was to help mitigate the spill impacts by acquiring coastal properties or hopefully clean-up the damages incurred from this horrible accident. As usual, humans clumsily try to undo damage we could have prevented in the first place.

MOUSE TIDBITS

Originally, the ABM were known as the White Fronted Beach Mouse and considered to be one of the smallest mammals in the world. The mice are about 5-6 inches long, no larger than a man's thumb, are covered with fur and are homoeothermic(warm blooded). Two large ears provide exceptional hearing and large black bulging eyes give them excellent vision. They have a keen sense of smell and their long white whiskers help them feel their way through small places. The mice's pale gray / brownish fur help make them almost invisible in a white, sandy world. A 2 inch tail with a brown stripe down the middle helps maintain their balance, while making quick maneuvers.

The mice form monogamous pairs and work together as a family, using parental cooperation in everything they do. Their average weight is 12.5 grams, with pregnant females averaging 20 gm. and the mice's reproductive potential is generally high. Once the female becomes pregnant, she carries the young for 23 days, and usually has 2-7 pups per litter, with an average of four. Newborn eyes and ears are sealed shut at birth, but open several days later.
After giving birth, the female is ready to mate within 24 hours, and this is important as the mortality rate of adult mice is also quite high. Young mice reach reproductive maturity as early as 6 weeks of age, and usually disperse and settle within one mile of their birthplace.

Beach mice in general, are nocturnal. They are more active during stormy conditions or moonless nights and less active on moonlit nights, because of predators. Their night outings are primarily for foraging for food, breeding and burrow maintenance. (Extine and Stout 1987) During daylight hours, they stay indoors in their uniquely constructed burrows, sleeping, eating and caring for their babies.

They have omnivorous appetites and eat both plant and
animal foods and gather seeds lying on the ground. During
spring, fall and winter months the mice collect a variety of
native seeds, which include sea oats, sea rocket, beach pea,
panic grass, blue stem, maritime grass, ground cherry,
evening primrose, dune spurge, joint weed, seashore elder,
and seaside pennywort. Acorns also provide a favorite from
the stunted oak tree areas closer to Mobile Bay, and during the
summer, insects of all types provide food.

The mice are fossorial, meaning they like to dig! While
digging a burrow the mouse assumes a straddling position to
dig the burrow and throws sand back between the hind legs
with the forefront. The hind feet are then used to kick sand
back while the mouse backs slowly up and out of the burrow,
(Ivey 1949)

Their spectacularly engineered burrows are found at the base
of the mature, sparsely vegetated primary and more densely
vegetated secondary dunes, other sandy vegetated areas and
even in swales, plus the sandy transition dwarfed tree areas. A
family may construct as many as 15-20 burrows in their
neighborhood home range and the spatial occupancy can
contain as many as 40-70 mice.

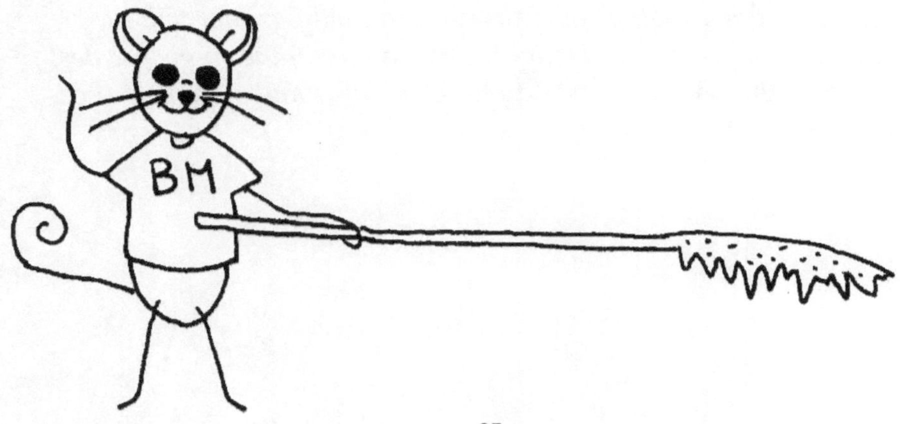

Bill Lynn of the USFWS offers Weber et al: *The burrow building ability of beach mice is an inherent genetic trait. An active burrow is characterized by a fan shaped plume of expelled sand found usually at the base of a dune. The 1-2 inch triangular opening of the entrance tunnel is flat at the base, rounded at the top, and camouflaged within clumps of grass or beneath sheltering vegetation, and is blocked with a series of sand plugs, presumably for predator defense. The small burrow extends three feet within the dune, and reeds or similar grass may be worked into the sloped edges of the tunnel offering stability. It contains 3 main chambers. The central chamber is the mice's bedroom and is filled with dried rush pads making great sleeping pads for Mom, Pop and the four to eight pups. A second chamber is for the storage of food and the third provides the escape hatch.*

The mouse has to be alert at all times because of numerous predators. Some of their predators are the great blue heron, great horned owl, weasel, red and grey fox, raccoon, coyote, striped skunk, bobcat, various snakes, including coach whip, pygmy, and diamondback rattlesnake, plus domestic dogs and cats.

D.W. Linzey sent me this: *Domestic cats are considered a global invasive species, as they kill 1.3 to 4.0 billion birds and 6.3 to 22.3 billion small mammals in the lower 48 states each year. Findings suggest that free-ranging cats cause substantially greater wildlife mortality than previously thought. They are likely the single greatest source of anthropogenic mortality for U.S. Birds and mammals (Loss et al 2013)*

There are many challenges in conducting effective and inexpensive monitoring, since footprints of small mice are not easily distinguishable. A classification tree was set up for distinguishing subspecies and species using front footprint widths. In the case of beach mice, they ranged between 5.5-6.7mm and cotton mice were 6.7- 8.3mm. The overall accuracy was approximately 94%
correct in classifying beach mouse and with less effort. (Journal of Fish & Wildlife Management, December 2018)

The ABM is an exceptionally smart mammal and is never the pest found in homes, buildings or garbage dumps. They have no reason for trusting people and are busy just trying to stay alive.

KEY-STONE SPECIES

An ecosystem is a biologically rich community of plants, birds, animals and vegetation that constantly work together to provide the necessities of life in a mutually beneficial manner. A disturbance within an ecosystem may involve key-stone specie, or one that is integral to its habitat.

The BM is certainly one, as it is an integral part of the dune system. One of their most important jobs is the gathering and storage of sea oat seeds. A few seeds will germinate within the burrow space and as the stalk of the new plant works up through the dune system, the maze of roots spread out helping to stabilize the system. In a locale as outwardly barren as the sandy beach it is conceivable that even the waste products from these tiny mammals may make a significant contribution for providing fertilizer for plant growth. Bottom line, if the mouse doesn't survive, the dune ecosystem will not.

ENVIRONMENTAL AWAKENNG

In the late 1960's it seemed as if overnight, there was a national environmental awakening. Families were sick and dying from the deadly, unregulated toxic pollution loads released in the air, waters, and stored in landfills. So, people got involved, joined forces and changed history. They woke Congress up to the seriousness of the problem and the first environmental legislation in the world was created.

The National Environmental Policy Act (NEPA) was passed in 1969 and was essentially the Magna Carta of environmental protection. It required federal agencies to prepare and release an Environmental Impact Statement (EIS), then strongly mandated public input and involvement usually during Public Hearings for all major proposed federal actions that might *significantly affect the quality of the human environment or threaten human health.*

NEPA was an environmental law with teeth, but other laws were desperately needed. Congress passed the Clean Air Act in 1970, which helped to protect the nation's air quality, promote and protect public health and welfare and the productive capacity of the population.

The Clean Water Act followed in 1972. Its purpose was to protect and restore the chemical, physical, and biological integrity of the Nation's waters. It was also intended to eliminate all discharges of pollution into the waters by 1985 and aspired to achieve fish-able, and swim-able waters, everywhere by 1983.

The Endangered Species Act (ESA) was passed in 1973, and President Nixon begrudgingly signed it into law. It created an absolute mandate: federal agencies will not jeopardize the continued existence of endangered or threatened species or adversely modify their habitat. The Act prohibits the *take or killing* of endangered species through direct harm and prevents critical habitat destruction in ecosystems on which they depend. This obviously includes the white sandy beaches and sand dunes of Baldwin County, the last habitat for the Alabama Beach Mouse.

Critical Habitat is a term which should be used cautiously, as it requires special management and protection. Major efforts need to be taken to include additional areas that are not currently occupied by the species, but will be needed for its continued recovery.

The ESA is jointly administered by the USFWS within the Department of the Interior (DOI). They are dedicated to overseeing management and protection of the threatened/endangered fish, wildlife and their habitats. Their vision is: *Together we will connect lands and waters to sustain fish, wildlife and plants by being visionary leaders, bold innovators and trusted partners, working with and for people.*

The other partner is the National Marine Fisheries Service (NMFS) within the National Ocean and Atmospheric Administration (NOAA), who oversee terrestrial and fresh water organisms. All of these laws are for the betterment of Mankind and the natural world. These four statutes form the bedrock of American environmental law!

The ESA has saved the ABM, so far. If any aspect of this interests you and you'd like to read more about environmental activism in Alabama you can read my book 'Chronicle of An Eco-Warrior Relating South Alabama's Environmental Issues.' It can be found on Amazon.

It vividly shows how private citizens, and a handful of politicians, created positive outcomes in all kinds of environmental battles in coastal Alabama. Remember, learning from the past means not making the same mistakes in the future. The following section drives home why people must stay vigilant, especially now a days!

DIRTY POLITICS

In 1982 Congress and others amended the ESA. This is a perfect example of dirty politics in action. The new Congressional ESA amendments authorized the USFWS, through the Secretary of the Interior, to issue permits for the incidental take of threatened and endangered wildlife species, under Section 10a (1) (B) of the ESA. Permit holders with an Incidental Takings Permit (ITP) could proceed with an activity that could result in affecting survival of any endangered specie, such as the ABM.

The 1982 amendment also required a permit applicant to *design, implement, and secure funding for a conservation plan or acquisition of property, which minimizes and mitigates harm to the impacted species, during the proposed project.*

That plan is commonly referred to as a Habitat Conservation Plan (HCP). A HCP is legally binding between the Secretary of Interior and the permit holder. The USFWS has to consider and approve a HCP, and the agency must be capable of properly enforcing the permit during the project.

We can't afford to ignore the Trump Administration. His cutting staff and funding for the environmental agencies and replacing Administrative positions with people of questionable backgrounds, makes it almost impossible to protect the coastal environment and human health. His choices have seriously weakened the federal agencies capability to properly oversee environmental threats by others, and have placed our coastal resources, human lives and wildlife in jeopardy...**AGAIN!**

BIODIVERSITY: FRAGMENTED HABITAT: RED LIST

Biodiversity is the variety of life on Planet Earth. Whole ecosystems contain and allow a wide variety of species to live and work together, within a specific environment. This cooperative effort not only boosts ecosystem productivity, but quickly becomes threatened, when badly planned mankind actions drastically change biodiversity at an unprecedented rate, in sensitive coastal areas. Habitat fragmentation during development and construction of new roads, plus the additional impacts from our toxic air and water pollution loads take their toll as well.

Fragmentation criss-crosses, degrades and destroys the mice's identified natural access/egress paths during the construction of more roads and development. These natural paths are vital for their survival; as during their daily travels in gathering food, the areas provide protection from the predators, allow dispersal of gene flow from one area to another supporting genetic diversity, which lessens inbreeding. All of these increase the mice's chance of survival.

The deadly pollution loads of non-regulated carbon, sulfur dioxide, plus other toxic pollutants released from smokestacks and our heavy traffic threaten not only human health and lives, but the lives and diversity of species, These and other man-made threats caused the ABM and others to be 'red-listed' and added to the Red List of Threatened Species on August 18, 2016

More than 26, 500 species are now threatened with extinction in the world, according to the International Union for Conservation of Nature (IUCN). The Red List of Threatened Species has become the world's most comprehensive information source on the global conservation status of animal, fungi and plant species. It is a critical indicator of the health of the world's biodiversity, and a powerful tool to inform and catalyze action for biological conservation and policy change, critical in protecting our natural resources, which citizens depend upon to survive.

Some of the Gulf state's flora and fauna have evolved to withstand the impacts of the tropical storms and hurricanes to some degree, but no species can withstand the impacts of man. Short-sighted planners, greedy developers and politicians in coastal Alabama and Florida seem to ignore any responsibility for recognizing the connectivity of man and Mother Nature; that could prove fatal to us as well.

DR. E.O. WILSON

Dr. E.O. Wilson, the world's renowned biologist, outlined in his book: The Diversity of Life what he considers as the four horsemen of the environmental apocalypse. All four have contributed to human alteration of the natural environment to the extent that the earth is now entering the sixth event of major extinctions. This is caused from:

1. Overexploitation
2. Habitat destruction
3. Introduction of alien species and diseases they carry
4. Pollution loads

Man depends utterly on the plants, animals and microorganisms of Earth. There should be real concern over species loss from destruction of habitat, over hunting, (predation in the beach mice's case), toxic air and water pollution, invasion by alien species and climate change. The resulting biological annihilation will have serious ecological, economic and social consequences for Mankind.

HUMANITY: GLOBAL SUPER PREDATORS: SIXTH EXTINCTION

Humanity is directly responsible for the sixth extinction event. We are such busy little destroyers that we can boast a current species extinction rate of 100 to 1,000 times higher than natural back ground rates. Ecologically, humanity has been called an unprecedented global super-predator and has affected every living species by either consuming it into extinction or polluting and crowding it out of existence. We must change.

POWER OF THE PEOPLE

First and foremost, we must change the way in which we view our responsibility to this planet. The good news is there are many conscientious individuals who are working hard to find solutions to our problems and the more you educate yourself about the perils facing our planet, the better able you are to help change them.

In past years, people became involved and enacted laws designed to protect the environment and human life from selfish politicians and greedy developers. These laws are now under attack by the government. All is not doom and gloom, as long as we are vigilant, stay informed, and involved, as there is still hope we can turn things around in time.

COASTAL ZONE MANAGEMENT PLAN: CZMP

In 1979, a proposed Coastal Zone Management Plan (CZMP) was presented the citizens attending a meeting in coastal Alabama. The only reason for the Plan was Senator Red Noonan and his cronies wanted Alabama to be considered as the candidate for an offshore oil port on the Gulf of Mexico and a CZMP was required. It was a huge disappointment, as the Plan only involved Mobile Bay.

After the meeting, members of the Mobile Bay Audubon Society organized a small group and three revisions were presented, before the Plan was finally accepted. The new comprehensive CZMP was one Alabamians could be proud of as it provided protection for our ecosystems as a whole. The Plan was expanded to include:

- Mobile Bay and adjacent rivers
- Mobile Tensaw Delta
- Mississippi Sound
- The Barrier Islands
- Gulf of Mexico and its unique invaluable beach and dune systems.

A Coastal Area Board (**CAB**) was set up and monthly meetings were held. A large number of citizens attended as there was very little trust for local politics!

HURRICANE FREDERIC CAME ALONG

Hurricane Frederic devastated Gulf Shores and Orange Beach in September 1979, becoming the first Category 4 hurricane since the 1930s. Winds were clocked at 145 mph, and storm surges ranged from 10-15' above normal. Five people were killed and large areas of dune systems and hundreds of structures were 'wiped out' along the Fort Morgan Peninsula.

GOVERNOR FOB JAMES

Immediately after the hurricane, the coastal area became a greed driven madhouse with loud threats of becoming 'condo land.' Governor Fob James with a single swipe of his pen completely wiped out the CZMP and the CAB. He then turned protection of our dunes, beach systems and wildlife over to the Alabama Economic Development Office (ADO), the enemy of our natural coastal resources.

Condominium developers must have been waiting in the shadows, as it seemed over-night men driving bulldozers were wreaking havoc in our dune systems, destroying sea oat plants, killing beach mice and any other creatures in their path. There was no monitoring of these activities, as everyone was in a hurry to build condos and make a bundle of money.

FEDERAL EMERGENCY MANAGEMENT AGENCY: FEMA

FEMA had just been established 3 months prior and became the overseer for the Federal Flood Insurance Program (FFIP). Damage from Hurricane Frederic cost taxpayers 2.3 billion dollars. This should have been an awakening for the taxpayer, as the program has now become a black-hole for their money. It just gets more expensive as the costs of the three hurricanes in 2017: Harvey, Irma and Maria totaled over 365 billion dollars!

The COC, Alabama politicians and developers helped pass the legislation, believing Alabama's coastal beach and dune areas should be developed at all costs. It's a mystery to me why some of the most morally bankrupt men and women on the planet are chosen for leadership roles.

ALABAMA DEPARTMENT OF ENVIRONMENTAL MANAGEMENT: ADEM

Joe Broadwater, a retired CIA agent, became Director of the Alabama Department of Environmental Management (ADEM), the state agency that is supposed to protect our coastal resources. They also oversee impacts on the environment...which is a joke. This person was an embarrassment to our state as seen by this quote from a newspaper article:

JOE BROADWATER:

QUOTE:*"I ain't no damn birdwatcher. What environment is it going to destroy if they go in and flatten the dunes? It's not going to do any great environmental harm. There are no endangered species in Baldwin County. It's not a breeding ground for sea oats or any endangered animal."* **END QUOTE**

Good for you, Joe! After all, what is the point in being stupid, unless you can prove it? But, despite this level of incompetent dumb ass found in Alabama politics there was a push-back from the more involved, enlightened portion of the population. Large tracts of land have now been saved from destruction due to the efforts of a few committed individuals.

A COASTAL REFUGE

Years ago Margaret Meade said that *People Power* is the most powerful force in the world and we proved her right, as a small group banded together and stopped the bulldozers...for a while!

Five members of the Mobile Bay Audubon Society, a representative from The Nature Conservancy, plus the USFWS became involved in the 1970's. We saved the first three major coastal properties that now make up the Bon Secour National Wildlife Refuge (BSNWR) in coastal Alabama. They are the Perdue Tract, Little Dauphin Island and Little Point Clear

Congress continues to receive credit for the existence of the BSNWR, but they only established the Refuge Bill, which provided funding needed to acquire the properties. They didn't seek out, set aside, promote or save the lands. Ordinary citizens did that and it's important for people to know that they can make things happen in this country, if they get involved!

1--PERDUE TRACT

As a young boy during the 1950's Skipper Tonsmiere and his young friend Ashley Perdue formed a deep personal attachment for a beautiful piece of coastal property on the Gulf of Mexico, called the Perdue Tract in Gulf Shores.

Twenty years later, as President of the Mobile Bay Audubon Society (MBAS) I received a call from Skipper, a member of the Society and building contractor in Baldwin County. He wanted to know how to save coastal lands and since I didn't know suggested he appear before the Audubon Board.

Skipper told the Board how he had been trying to save the Perdue property for many years without any luck. The tract consisted of approximately 1,400 acres on the Gulf of Mexico and had originally been purchased in1920 for a little over $1 per acre by W.W. Perdue, the founder of Ace Hardware. In 1973 it was sold to Fletcher Properties, a developer. An engineer from Florida, representing the owner, approached Skipper, about doing some building for them at Gulf Shores. He was appalled while looking at their plans and the utter devastation planned for the property and wanted to do something to stop it, but didn't know how.

His presentation impressed everyone but especially:

- John Borom, an educator
- Nancy Garrett, a biologist and housewife
- Jack Friend, member of the Mobile Chamber of Commerce
- and Me

The five of us were ready to save the property, but a developer held an option on it, so our hands were tied. Not knowing how to proceed I called Mary Burks, a dear friend, who headed up The Alabama Conservancy in Birmingham. She had been involved in saving properties in north Alabama and suggested that I contact Dave Morine. He was the National Land Acquisition VP for The Nature Conservancy. David knew of the property, quickly joined our small force and encouraged us to work with the USFWS, as the federal agency was involved and very interested in this coastal parcel.

Skipper took us on a tour of the Perdue Tract and we marveled over the 8,000 feet of 'untouched' beautiful white sandy beaches on the Gulf of Mexico. There were healthy dune systems, a portion of Little Lagoon, and two freshwater Gator Lakes containing untouched Indian middens, acres of mixed forests, wetlands and forested swamps. All of this provided food, shelter, nesting, feeding, safety, nursery and foraging areas for a variety of abundant birdlife, terrestrial, marine life and of course, the ABM.

DEVELOPER'S PLANS

When I saw the developer's plans tears filled my eyes! An eighteen-hole golf course, condominiums and multiple houses were to be constructed throughout the sensitive acreage, along with a shopping center, a maze of concrete roads, parking spaces, tennis courts and infrastructure needs.

MIGRATORY FLYWAYS

The USFWS surprised everyone by doing what is called 'A Quick Study' to determine whether the 1,400 acre coastal property met the stiff requirements for acquisition through the Migratory Bird Act of 1918. The property was situated on two of the four migratory flyways that crossed the Gulf of Mexico. The tract passed the needed requirements with flying colors and this was good news.

DEVELOPER LOSES OPTION

Luckily, the developer lost his option on the property, so before other developers could snatch it up I called the Chase Manhattan of New York and was informed the sale price was ten million dollars. I quickly called Dave Morine, who told me not to worry, as The Nature Conservancy would buy and hold the 1,400 acres. They eventually paid 4.8 million dollars.

MYRT'S NOTE: NO FEDERAL INTERVENTION

We were extremely lucky to save these lands as not many people know that Alabama is the only state along the Gulf Coast that doesn't have a National Seashore. The story goes that a small group of powerful local 'rich' men, working behind the scenes, met the Washington Representative at the Mobile municipal airport and told him to stay on the plane. They didn't want *any federal intervention in the State of Alabama.* Those of us trying to save lands in the corrupt state of Alabama, and especially in the coastal area, heard *no federal intervention* frequently during the 70's and 80's, but for some unknown reason these coastal parcels were to be acquired and saved by US!

Other citizen's efforts were thwarted by these same greedy men. The MBAS and Tom Davis of Sunshine Canoes tried to place the Escatawpa River in the Wild & Scenic Rivers Bill, but were stopped. During the final Public Hearing, Jay P Altmayer, Scott and International Paper Mills, three major property owners on the river, opposed the listing. Jay P. tapped me on the shoulder and laughingly announced he was the one who had stopped me. I told him what I thought of him.

Our efforts for placing the Mobile-Tensaw Delta in the Wildlife Refuge or a National Sanctuary were also stymied by these same ignorant, short sighted greedy individuals, who believed they ruled Alabama. It's our job as citizens to try and neutralize their toxicity.

2--LITTLE DAUPHIN ISLAND: LDI

The USFWS weren't finished, and now were focused on acquiring Little Dauphin Island (LDI), which is on the west side of Mobile Bay, in Mobile County. It is the only north-south barrier island along the northern Gulf Coast. The small ecosystem contains 838 acres, and lies 11 feet above sea level. It consists of beautiful white sandy beaches and sparse forests with medium pine tree coverage.

Dauphin Island Bay provides invaluable brackish water and prime submerged bottom lands, containing acres of precious salt marsh and tidal flats, as well as cultural archeological Indian relics, from years past. A variety of migratory and shorebirds use these coastal resources, as well as marine invertebrates and vertebrates.

Before going on let's inject a little bit of unknown history. In the early 70's members of the MBAS became involved in a Corps of Engineers Public Notice, and actually saved these precious lands from destruction. A Corps permit had been requested by Anderson Corporation, Inc. for a major dredge and fill operation, that would wipe out Dauphin Island Bay and its bottom lands, surface waters, prime marsh and wetlands, for a medical conference center. Members discovered the company had lied, as the Ford Foundation was not supporting the project, and the permit was denied. People involvement saved these invaluable coastal resources from destruction.

Chris Delaney was the owner of Little Dauphin Island and wanted the property placed in the Refuge, but had made an agreement with the State Highway Department (SHD). They were constructing the Dauphin Island Bridge, following Hurricane Frederick's devastation, and he had requested a ramp be constructed from it to the island. I told Chris the Audubon Society wouldn't support acquiring the parcel if a ramp was on it, so he cancelled the agreement with SHD, and LDI became the second tract in the BSNWR. Precious things come in small packages and the 838 acres were finally purchased by The Nature Conservancy for $1,158,660.00.

3--LITTLE POINT CLEAR: LPC

The last parcel on their list was Little Point Clear. This exceptionally beautiful, lush coastal property juts out into Mobile Bay on the north side of Fort Morgan Peninsula. It consists of several small pristine inter-tidal river inlets, contains high quality maritime forested swamps, brackish water wetlands, scrub oak dunes and sand dune beach habitats.

It is rich with a variety of birds, marine life, mammals, reptiles and many endangered and threatened species, including the ABM. More than 370 species of birds have been identified during migratory seasons and that includes shorebirds and wetland dependent species. They use this prime coastal habitat for nesting, feeding, resting, foraging and wintering.

The parcel became a battleground as Roger Page, an oilman and owner, intended to canalize the natural river systems, dredge, fill and destroy huge acreage of wetlands and swamps, then develop the area with Florida style homes. His plan involved structurally controlling the shorelines of the rivers by bulk heading their banks, so the residents could dock boats, next to their homes.

Other environmental groups along with state and federal agencies had now joined forces in giving their support, as it was a well-known fact that the property was a top priority for the Refuge. Mr. Page was rather greedy, as a few years earlier, Skipper and friends had made an offer of $3 million for the property, but Page turned it down saying his bottom line was $10 million dollars.

His permits were denied and Page ran into a financial mess, finally selling 500 acres in 1979 to The Nature Conservancy for $500,000.00, becoming the third and final parcel for the BSNWR. These three parcels were the largest undeveloped tracts of land and dunes that have ever been acquired in perpetuity on Alabama's coast and are now priceless coastal treasures. The efforts of a hand full of people paid off as:

- these natural systems are now protected in perpetuity
- they provide shelter and food for numerous species
- act as natural buffers against frequent storms
- provide educational, scientific, and recreational opportunities
- It's there for future generations to enjoy.

These precious acres are a reminder of how the Gulf Coast was before development. They now preserve the natural habitat vital for all of the numerous threatened and endangered species living there, and that includes the ABM.

BON SECOUR NATIONAL WILDLIFE REFUGE: BSNWR

The USFWS appealed to Congress to set up the Congressional Refuge Bill, which would provide funds to acquire them and properly set aside lands to be saved. Alabama Congressmen Jack Edwards and Senator Howell Heflin co-sponsored and pushed the bill through Congress.

On June 9, 1980, President Jimmy Carter signed the Bon Secour Bill, making it **A REALITY** and the first of its kind for coastal Alabama!

The Bon Secour National Wildlife Refuge Bill: conserves the well-being of the undisturbed coastal beach/dune systems, ensures and protects the nationally threatened and endangered species, preserves an ecosystem that includes a diversity of fish, wildlife and their habitats, serves as an outdoor living laboratory for students, scientists and provides wildlife-oriented recreation compatible with recreational opportunities for the public.

This was quite an achievement, as volunteers saved and helped acquire all three properties, and became the first land acquisition of its kind, for the citizens and wildlife of coastal Alabama. These three acquisitions comprised of 2,738 acres had been purchased for a total of $6,458,660.00.

The Refuge staff now oversee and protects these unique habitats and associated wildlife for us and generations to come, using a variety of habitat management techniques in maintaining, recovering or enhancing plant and wildlife values. They believe the greatest challenges posed for managing the Bon Secour Refuge are the declining populations of fish & wildlife species and loss of habitat to development, which accelerates species decline.

When you visit the Gulf for a vacation, make it a point to visit the BSNWR with the understanding these properties would now be filled with condos, golf courses and shopping centers, if not for a small force of private citizens, becoming involved and making it happen.

A NICE COMPLIMENT

It's nice to be appreciated. In 1986 David Morine of The
Nature Conservancy was the major speaker during the
dedication of the Weeks Bay National Estuarine Research
Reserve. He surprised me with one of the nicest compliments
I've received during my many years of volunteerism/
involvement.

He said that The Nature Conservancy would only consider
buying property from willing sellers and if it wasn't for
people like me, who recognized unique threatened areas, and
used persuasion or other means to open the door for his
organization, then few lands would be acquired. He likened
me to the individuals in World War Two, who cast their
bodies across the barbed wire in order to allow the next force
to capture the objective. I have enough invisible psychic scars
to know he's right.

LOBBYING

Learning how to lobby may become a necessity if a person
wants to become an involved citizen, activist, or
conservationist. In the early 1980's twenty volunteers attended
the National Audubon Society's first lobbying workshop held
in Washington. Brock Evans and Connie Mahan and their staff
directed us towards using scientific facts and natural reasons
for arguing the need to renew the ESA and the CWA. It was
great fun, and many of our points actually helped sway some
Congressmen's support our way!

CONGRESSMAN JACK EDWARDS

Congressman Jack Edwards became a regular contact during
my early days of lobbying on environmental issues.
Originally, he was seen as a pork barrel type of Congressman,
meaning he supported extremely costly, destructive
environmental boondoggles such as the Tenn Tom-Waterway,
but we could always openly discuss issues in a friendly
manner. One day he surprised me by sharing his concerns
about his legacy and what his grandsons may think when they
read his Congressional voting record. We discussed the ways
he might become a more environmentally friendly politician,
starting with his involvement in the BSNWR.

ANOTHER NEAT CONGRESSMAN: SENATOR HOWELL HEFLIN

Senator Howell Heflin was another enjoyable contact and one
Alabamian's could be proud of knowing and voting for. One
day, after rushing to catch up with him in the long hallway of
Congress, I was just able to grab hold of the tail of his coat. He
turned around, continuing to puff on his cigar and said, "Well,
young lady, since you have caught me, what can I do for
you?" I told him, 'A group of us had saved the first coastal
property in Gulf Shores and The Nature Conservancy
acquired the tract and was holding it. It was imperative for
Congress to pass the Refuge bill.' He replied "Whatever Jack
wants, I'll support." Congressman Jack Edwards and Senator
Howell Heflin co-sponsored the bill, helped establish the Act,
and these wonderful coastal lands were now saved.

LITIGATION MADE A TREMENDOUS DIFFERENCE

The following legal battles show the need for and benefits of using court actions for saving coastal lands, protecting lives and species in Alabama. The first one resulted in an out-of-court settlement that set-up the Alabama Coastal Heritage Trust Fund (ACHTF). This Fund helped acquire additional coastal lands for the BSNWR.

The other court cases helped protect the mice and their habitat in causing lengthy delays, which resulted in project changes and acquisition. People should thank the judges and lawyers involved in these legal cases. They actually "lay across the barb wire" by enforcing laws, which now protect our lives, property and creatures. Hopefully, these lawsuits have instilled a deeper respect and need for protecting fragile habitats in high coastal energy areas.

MORRILL VS LUJAN & PERDIDO KEY BM

The first endangered beach mouse litigation was Morrill vs. Lujan and was filed on October 31, 1991, by Dr. Joy Morrill, a local Marine Biologist. She grew up in Cotton Bayou and was concerned that no one seemed to be protecting our coast.

Hank Caddell, was the Plaintiff's attorney and was assisted by Birmingham attorney Bob Reid, a member of the Birmingham Audubon Society. Caddell claimed that the government dropped the ball by not enforcing the ESA, as the mouse and their habitat was seriously threatened. He stated that the ESA is not worth the paper it's written on if the government is going to ignore their responsibility.

The suit temporarily stopped construction of a hotel and 600 parking spaces. The project threatened many of the last remaining dunes and critical habitat of the Perdido Key Beach Mouse in Orange Beach, Alabama. After a year, the litigant's funds ran out and they were unable to appeal, but the developer came forward with a settlement offer. He offered a fund to be set up to protect the mouse along with major commitments for making the project more mice friendly. The case was settled out of court and the Alabama Coastal Heritage Trust Fund (ACHTF) was born.

Article in the Mobile Register, June 29, 1992…"he is so powerful that because of him, instead of being open for business, only a skeleton of a multi-million dollar restaurant and lounge stands on the property of Perdido Key at Orange beach."

Jim Trippe with the Environmental Defense Fund reported that the beach mouse was nearing extinction in 1979, and had been declared an endangered species in 1985. He said that if it quietly dies on the REDNECK RIVIERA it shows there is no backbone to the ESA,

MARTINIQUE & BEACH CLUB: ABM

On March 5, 1997, the Fort Morgan Civic Association, the Sierra Club and Mickey Stephens filed a letter of intent to sue Bruce Babbitt, then Secretary of The Department of the Interior (DOI). He was directed to withdraw the Incidental Takings Permit (ITP) to Martinique, as they planned a complex of condos and homes on 52 acres of land surrounded by the BSNWR.

The Beach Club was a Wolf Creek Industries project and their proposed construction on 86 acres consisted of 753 condo units, houses, duplexes, commercial buildings, pools, tennis courts, roads, parking lots, and infrastructure needs. It was to be built on the very sand dunes, which provided habitat for the beach mice, as the property was immediately adjacent to the BSNWR

Among these consecutively granted ITP's were two other high-density nearby developments: Laguna Key and **Kiva Dunes (see article below)**. Applications had been submitted for an oceanfront golf course in the residential community and construction of an 84 unit condominium.

The USFWS violated their official recovery plan, which stated that maintaining and improving the remaining habitat is essential for mouse survival, as fewer than 900 of the small mice remain on less than 350 acres of habitat. Since the plan was written 18% of that habitat has been destroyed by hurricanes and development yet the USFWS still issued ITP's.

The Sierra Club alleged that the USFWS consistently violated their own rules in granting the ITP's for the Martinique and Beach Club projects, as well as several others within the sand dunes near Fort Morgan. These permits would allow habitat to be destroyed and mice killed during construction, jeopardizing the continued existence of the ABM.

The Service supported the developers Habitat Conservation Plan (HCP) but did not require the permit holders to acquire additional beach mouse habitat to compensate for the lands they take. The ESA requires the USFWS to develop and implement recovery plans in a HCP, and include actions necessary to prevent extinction and assure conservation and recovery of the species. The idea is to get the populations healthy enough, so that they no longer need Federal protection, yet somehow the Martinique complex exists with the following conditions:

-- Boardwalks were required to the beach
-- Persons were prohibited from disturbing habitat
-- Restrictive covenants to minimize predators
-- A lighting plan that avoids illuminating critical habitat
-- Approval for planting of plants
-- Funds for trapping and monitoring house mice
   populations and feral cats
-- Funds to acquire additional lands, educational signs and
   brochures to inform others of the mouse.

MORE SHENANIGANS: KIVA DUNES

Excerpts from Lagniappe's article "Conservation litigation," Federal lawsuit claims Baldwin appraiser gave 'sham' valuations…by Gabriel Tynes …March 13, 2017 involving Kiva Dunes

The complaint claims Claud Clark III of Magnolia Springs appraised at least 187 conservation easements between 2009 and 2016, including at least 58 for syndicates. It further alleges the partners in those 58 syndicates reported more than $1.85 billion in "grossly overstated" federal tax deductions, leading the Treasury Department to suffer "losses through tax refunds wrongfully issued and taxes uncollected in an amount yet to be fully determined."

Perhaps the most publicized of those appraisals was Kiva Dunes, a resort community and golf course on the Fort Morgan peninsula that was granted a conservation easement in 2002. When Clark's appraisal of Kiva Dunes was challenged and upheld in U.S. Tax Court in 2009, it awarded a $31 million tax break to grantor D&E Investments. This LLC incorporation by husband and wife Elbert Allen ("Larry") and Abbie Drummond, were heirs to the coal mining Drummond Company. In tax court, the IRS argued the property was only worth $10 million.

The Lagniappe article continues …A 2009 story in the Press-Register about the court's decision in the case began, "Appraiser Claud Clark doesn't often invent a fake subdivision just to establish land values, but that's what he did to the Kiva Dunes Golf Course on Fort Morgan." The reader can refer to the Lagniappe article for further information.

GULF HIGHLANDS & BEACH CLUB WEST: ABM

In April of 2002, Gulf Highlands and Beach Club West on Fort Morgan Peninsula were enjoined by the Mobile Federal Court. The case focused on the failure of USFWS to analyze the potential for impacts on the beach mouse. Seven projects, which included condominiums, homes, commercial buildings, parking lots, pools, tennis courts, and infrastructure, were planned in the midst of beach mouse habitat. The federal judge was asked to allow additional analysis, a legal process, which went on for almost five years.

On May 31, 2007 Judge William Steele in the Alabama Federal Court issued a preliminary injunction, which prevented any action that resulted in killing the ABM, until a final decision could be reached in the case. Judge Steele's decision highlighted just how crucial every remaining acre of high elevation habitat is to the endangered species.

For the second time, Cynthia Sarthou, Executive Director of the Gulf Restoration Network, Sierra Club and Center for Biological Diversity challenged the USFWS findings. The challengers stated that destruction of 40 acres of key beach mouse habitat for the resorts would drive the species closer to extinction. A significant portion of the habitat that would be destroyed was the rare high-elevation habitat necessary for the species to survive hurricanes. As little as 128 acres (or one-fifth) of the high-elevation habitat would remain above water in a Category 5 hurricane, possibly pushing the ABM species closer to extinction.

In 2009, another attempt was made by the developers to continue the project, but thanks to Federal Judge Steele, the controversial multi-million dollar condo was stopped again, just hours before bull-dozers were set to begin mowing down sand dunes and mouse burrows. He had read the Finding of No Significant Impacts (FONSI), from NEPA, a critical federal document where the USFWS had likely reached arbitrary and capricious conclusions during the process, which would result in the killing of the ABM. The Judge issued a preliminary injunction, which prevented any further action, until a final decision could be made….and that could take several months?

Sierra Club attorney Robert Wiygul said, "If there's any lesson that I hope people learned from this case, it's better to go and get these things out to the public and perhaps even listen to what the people are saying."

ALAMAMA GOVERNORS ARE NOT ABOVE THE LAW

In 2016 Governor Robert Bentley believed he was above the Law of the Land, especially in Alabama. His complete abandonment of responsibility should not have astounded anyone, as he had just lost his beach residence in a recent divorce.

Bentley showed complete fiscal irresponsibility, and total disrespect for Alabama's coastal resources and creatures, plus the people he worked for in the state. He was discovered using BP's monies to restore the moldy Governor's Mansion, which had been destroyed by Hurricane Danny in 1997. He completely ignored citizen suggestions to use the funds to acquire bay-front property for a much needed public park, on Mobile Bay.

The Governor did not have permits for building his eight foot high, sixty foot long concrete wall, which blocked public access to state-owned beaches. No-one in the Governor's office had requested an ITP or HCP permits from the USFWS for His wall, which encroached on the ABM's habitat and violated the ESA. He was finally made to tear it down, but Bentley typifies the sort of corrupt, dumbass leadership commonly found in Alabama.

ACQUISITIONS: GULF HIGHLANDS TRACT

In 2016 the NFWF responded to a request from Hank Caddell for an award of $37,957,100 to be placed in the ACHTF. This was used to acquire and preserve the Gulf Highlands Tract on the Fort Morgan Peninsula. The parcel had been involved in lengthy litigation actions for years. After acquiring the property it was deeded to the Alabama Department of Conservation & Natural Resources, State Parks Division for long-term management and limited access in Ft. Morgan Parkway's Management Area,

This beautiful coastal property contains 113 acres with 2,700 feet of prime beaches and some of the highest dune systems ranging between 15'- 20' found along Alabama's coast. The parcel's proximity to the BSNWR enhances both properties' value, as it provides critical beachfront habitat for a variety of coastal birds and critters, such as the piping plover, sea turtles and the endangered ABM, in perpetuity.

NAVY COVE

In 2017, Ray Herndon of The Conservation Fund (TCF) and Jeremy Phillips, Refuge Complex Manager with the USFWS in Daphne, used $5,914,900.00 of funds from the NFWF. This provided for the purchase of two hundred and fifty one acres of sensitive coastal property on the Fort Morgan Peninsula, known as the Navy Cove parcel, within Little Point Clear Unit. This sensitive coastal system includes scrub/shrub, pine flat-wood, saltwater marsh, and tidal creek habitats, plus permanent and semi-permanent wetlands scattered across the parcel. It was finally acquired and saved after years of lawsuits with developers, then transferred to the BSNWR

THREE RIVERS

In 2018, Ray Herndon of The Conservation Fund received
$4,423,000.00 from the NFWF and acquired 236 acres of
estuarine forested shrub wetlands. This property is identified
as Three Rivers in the Little Point Clear Unit, and is bordered
on the east, west and north by Bon Secour Bay. It was
transferred to the USFWS, becoming part of the BSNWR.

The tract had been identified by the USFWS as being amongst
the highest priority for acquisition, as well as conservation
and providing long term management in the BSNWR's
Comprehensive Conservation Plan. It was specifically
included in the Mobile Bay National Estuary Program's Bon
Secour, Oyster Bay, and Skunk Bayou Watershed
Management Plan, as a priority for habitat protection.

ACQUISITIONS BY SIERRA CLUB

Tom Hodges, Chapter President of the Alabama Sierra Club,
Coastal Chapter turned over $835,000.00 of settlement monies
to the ACHT. The monies had been received from litigation
actions against the proposed Gulf Highlands developer and
these properties were later added to the BSNWR:

- In 2005: the 40 sq. acre PCS parcel, wholly within Unit 2
  of the BSNWR at Little Point Clear had been bought by
  the owners 40 years before in the hopes of building a
  sewage plant. It was acquired for $550,000.00

- In 2007: the 5.1 acre Saltwater Parcel within Unit 1 of
  the BSNWR (Perdue Tract) along the Dixie Hwy was
  bought for around $330.000.00 by ACHT then added to
  BSNWR

Since 2010 ACHT has been designated by the USFWS to receive and administer incidental take permit fees assessed for Ft. Morgan in the Critical Habitat of the ABM. Thus far, ACHT has received around $700,000.00 to be used for the preservation of beach and dune habitat, acquisition of conservation easements, planting of sea oats, etc.

Hopefully the reader realizes the first lawsuit was filed by local individuals to protect the Perdido Key Beach Mouse. Following that, the Sierra Club, Gulf Restoration Network, Center for Biological Diversity and numerous others took on badly planned projects that threatened the coastal resources and ABM. These groups stayed on top of proposed projects for years, as developer's continued to threaten Alabama's priceless coastal resources and endangered species, with their badly planned high density destructive development in high risk coastal zones.

Special thanks go to Judge Steele's efforts in legally helping to stop the madness on Fort Morgan Peninsula. The Judge's legal concerns helped protect Alabama's coastal areas from becoming another Miami or Houston.

Special interests shouldn't be allowed to win over public interest all of the time and these wins show how people involvement saved places for current and future generations. It's called stewardship.

LET'S DISCUSS HURRICANES

OPAL

On October 4, 1995, Hurricane Opal tore into BSNWR in Gulf Shores, Alabama as a Category 4. The maximum sustained winds ranged from 115-150 mph. There were numerous tornadoes and the rainfall was estimated to be over 19 inches. Falling trees caused 8 deaths along Alabama/ Florida's coasts.

Opal's devastating storm surges inundated portions of the

Florida Panhandle coast up to 10-20 ft. The powerful winds, salt water storm surges and strong waves flattened the sand dunes and the facilities in the Gulf State Park, leaving only the walk-over in place. Damage ranged in the billions.

EXCERPTS FROM SCIENTIFIC STUDY: OPAL

The following excerpts are from a Scientific Study focused on Hurricane Opal's Impacts on the ABM Populations: Importance of Deep Dune Systems on Gulf Coast Beaches… Holler, Wooten-(ACFWRU1) 1-3-1996

At the time two Choctawhatchee BM populations existed, one group at Topsail Hill near Destin, Fla. and another on Shell Island, east of Panama City Beach. The Perdido Key BM was at Gulf State Park on Perdido Key, Alabama, and the ABM's small populations at Fort Morgan and BSNWR. ABM's population had been reduced by Hurricane Elena in 1985 and losses were most severe at Fort Morgan Historical Park. The Perdido Key BM population at Gulf Islands had been wiped out by Hurricane Frederic in the 70s.

Opals' storm surges and heavy waves caused extensive damage to secondary dune fields in Alabama and Florida with a lot of flooding behind the dunes, drowning some mice while others dying from lack of food and shelter. The Bon Secour population was in the best shape, because of the Refuge's deep dune system, one of the best remaining on the Gulf Coast.

Dune habitats, and the mice quickly recovered from previous storm damage within three years after the ACFWSU projects were initiated and substantial populations of all 3 subspecies were established along the coasts. Mice remained in the secondary and the scrub dune systems, as they provide additional and safer habitat.

The researchers usually hesitate to intervene, but these folks assisted the USFWS and National Park Service, in spreading sun flower seeds in the Fort Morgan, Florida Point and Gulf Islands National Seashore, to sustain remaining mice

Holler/Wooten, a geneticist, hope to compare pre- and post-hurricane genetic attributes to determine if populations have suffered a loss of genetic material that might reduce potential for long-term survival.

Why care if they survive? Protecting the BM from extinction is important for a variety of reasons. The first is the aesthetic value of all life… many consider reason enough… they are important to the coastal ecosystem… actually benefit humanity and provide scientific information. Most obvious lessons learned from Opal is importance of the entire sand dune system is to the wildlife along the Gulf Coast, and how vital it is to preserve entire dune systems, not just the frontal ones.

IVAN

Hurricane Ivan made landfall at 2 am September 16, 2004, as a Category 5, making a direct hit on Gulf Shores, Alabama. It was the strongest hurricane to hit Baldwin County in more than 100 years and the worst one for the 2004 Atlantic season, in terms of coastal sand and land loss.

The majority of Alabama and Florida's frontal dunes disappeared and salt water surges inundated the mice's burrows causing populations to drop to 60 %. Sea turtle nests were destroyed. There were extensive damages with 123 fatalities, plus insured losses were above 26 billion dollars.

The BSNWR suffered extensive damage from Ivan's 20-foot storm surges and a great deal of wildlife habitat was destroyed. The Jeff Friend Trail suffered damages and the Pine Beach Trail System lost both the Gator Lake boardwalk and observation pavilion. Following debris removal, repairs and the replacement of the boardwalk, both trails were reopened to the public. The dunes of the Perdue unit suffered extensive damage, but natural processes are beginning to repair the damage. Rainfall in the coastal areas of Mobile and Pensacola was recorded at 9 to 16 inches.

Average shoreline erosion between Alabama's Mobile Bay and Florida's Pensacola Bay was 42' in areas, where Ivan came ashore. Structures in the Gulf State Park in the Gulf Shores area were flattened and the suitable habitat for the mice was reduced from 90 acres to zero.

Efforts to reintroduce the ABM within the Gulf State Park were initiated in 2010, with the transplanting of eleven mating mice from an existing population. The USFWS regularly monitored the population and concluded that the repopulation had been successful.

KATRINA

Hurricane Katrina was a Category 5 Hurricane that hit the Gulf coast on August 29, 2005. The 175 mph winds, high waters and heavy surges helped salt water intrusion degrade drinking water supplies and heavily impacted vegetation. Katrina's winds, surges, floods, torrential rains, and salt water destroyed primary and secondary dunes and vegetation, killed mice and other species, demolished homes, caused 1,836 fatalities and did 125 billion dollars in destruction and damages.

The ABM was almost extinct from the combined damages of Ivan and Katrina, as 90-95% of their habitat and food sources were destroyed. Following these catastrophes, the USFWS developed methods to restore the land using Dune Restoration Workshops. These provided the public opportunities to learn about native vegetation replenishment on their properties. Because of these and other efforts the populations of ABM returned to pre-hurricane numbers.

HELP PROTECT THE BM

Folks, you can make a difference. Give your time to help nature and protect the environment. Be a person who cares about the world you live in as every little bit helps:

- Avoid walking in or on the fragile dunes, use the designated boardwalks or walk around them
- Do not drive any vehicle such as dune buggies in or on dunes, dune vegetation, near or on beach areas
- Keep pets out of dunes. Dogs on leashes and cats indoors
- Create and cultivate an environmentally friendly home
- Plant native plants such as sea oats.
- Be respectful. Dispose of trash properly.
- Use rodent-proof garbage cans with tight fitting lids.
- Vote for political candidates who actively support the environment. Become a gadfly.
- Keep outdoor lights to a minimum or off
- Become an activist. Join an environmental organization e.g. NRDC, Sierra, Audubon or Defenders of Wildlife.
- Don't use rodenticides or pesticides in coastal areas
- Avoid using snap traps, glue boards and similar techniques outdoors in beach mouse habitat
- Do not feed outdoor feral cats in beach mouse habitat.

BECOME CITIZEN WATCHDOGS!

There is a definite need for citizen watchdogs throughout the Nation, but especially in coastal Alabama, as the USFWS Office in Daphne continue to receive numerous requests for Building Permits in ABM habitat. This can provide an important opportunity for people involvement and input. The Service currently use conservation efforts and eyes future planning needs for the mice in these unique coastal systems, and hopefully will increase survival odds for the mouse and other species.

Coastal areas have a unique diversity of wildlife and beautiful sensitive natural resources, many of which continue to be threatened by Man and Nature. They play an important role in the Earth's Fragile Closed Webs of Life, and must be respected and protected, not just for us, but for future generations.

Condos crowd the Orange Beach sand
Where few houses stood before,
The windswept dunes still stand
Firm in sea oats along the shore.

We walk quietly arm in arm,
In the crisp morning air,
Trying not to alarm
Small creatures scurrying there.

It's ours to enjoy only now,
And not trash like some,
But secure such places somehow
For the benefit of generations to come.

Then they, in turn, can wander,
Through and make this splendor last,
Respectful of these lovely areas
That are dwindling much too fast.

**Poem by Myrt's brother,
Dr. John S. Taylor, November 11, 1991**

REFERENCES

<u>Myrt's Notes</u>

Carrington, Damian. "Earth's Sixth Mass Extinction Event under Way, Scientists Warn." *The Guardian*, Guardian News and Media, 10 July 2017, **www.theguardian.com/environment/2017/jul/10/earths-sixth-mass-extinction-event-already-underway-scientists-warn**.

"Uniola Paniculata." *Wikipedia*, Wikimedia Foundation, 19 June 2018, **en.wikipedia.org/wiki/Uniola_paniculata**.
Young, Debbie, and Wildlife Service. "Daphne Ecological Services Field Station." *Greater Sage-Grouse | Species Information*, **www.fws.gov/daphne/**.
"Alabama Beach Mouse." *Wikipedia*, Wikimedia Foundation, 15 June 2018, **en.wikipedia.org/wiki/Alabama_beach_mouse**.

U.S. Fish & Wildlife Service. "Species Profile for Alabama Beach Mouse (PeromyscusPolionotusAmmobates)." *Listed Species Count by Year*, **ecos.fws.gov/ecp0/profile/speciesProfile?spcode=A08Y**.
Wooten, Michael C. "Alabama Beach Mouse." *Outdoor Alabama*, **www.outdooralabama.com/rodents/alabama-beach-mouse**.

Hoekstra, Hopi E., et al. "A Single Amino Acid Mutation Contributes to Adaptive Beach Mouse Color Pattern." *Science*, American Association for the Advancement of Science, 7 July 2006, **science.sciencemag.org/content/313/5783/101.full**.

Weber, Jesse N., et al. "Discrete Genetic Modules Are
    Responsible for Complex Burrow Evolution in
    Peromyscus Mice." *Nature News*, Nature Publishing
    Group, 16 Jan. 2013,
    www.nature.com/articles/nature11816.

"Alabama Beach Mouse - PeromyscusPolionotusAmmobates -
    Details." *Encyclopedia of Life*,
    eol.org/pages/1225979/details.

Powell, Kris. "Saving the Smallest of Endangered Species-The
    Beach Mouse." *Kris-Powell*, 16 Feb. 2015,
    **www.krislpowell.com/saving-smallest-endangered-
    species-beach-mouse/**.

Chapman, Dan. "The Mouse That Roared." *Greater Sage-
    Grouse | Species Information*, 13 Dec. 2017,
    **www.fws.gov/southeast/articles/the-mouse-that-
    roared/**.

Bird, Brittany L., et al. "Beach Mice." *EDIS New Publications
RSS*, School of Forest Resources and Conservation, 16 Mar.
2016, **edis.ifas.ufl.edu/uw173**.

Milligan, Neil S. "OF MICE AND HUMANS." *The Harbinger.
    Knowing the Human Genome: The Impact on Society*,
    www.theharbinger.org/xv/970304/neil.html.

GrrlScientist. "Never Say Goodbye: Alabama Beach Mouse."
    Cognitive Daily, 26 Jan. 2009,
    **scienceblogs.com/grrlscientist/2009/01/26/never-say-
    goodbye-alabama-beac/**.

Rogers, Jeanne E. "LIFE'S A BEACH." *AUSTRALIAN FANTASY ADVENTURES*, 19 Jan. 2016, **warriorechidna.blogspot.com/2016/01/lifes-beach-when-were-on-beach-we-dont.html**.

Fleshler, David. "Gray Foxes Thrive in South Florida -- but Are Rarely Seen." *Sun-Sentinel.com*, 25 Nov. 2015, **www.sun-sentinel.com/local/fl-urban-foxes-20151125-story.html**.

Miller, Phil. "Bobcat." *Outdoor Alabama*, **www.outdooralabama.com/carnivores/bobcat**.

"North American Bird Migration: The 4 Flyways." *Birdfeeder*, **www.perkypet.com/articles/north-american-bird-migration-4-flyways**.

"Bird Migration: Birds of the Mississippi Flyway." *Birdfeeder*, **www.perkypet.com/articles/mississippi-flyway-migration**.

U.S. Fish and Wildlife Service,. "Endangered Species Permits." *Greater Sage-Grouse | Species Information*, 26 Feb. 2018, **www.fws.gov/midwest/endangered/permits/hcp/index.html**.

John Wiley & Sons Ltd. "Conservation of Island Flora and Fauna." *Encyclopedia of Life Sciences*, Aug. 2016, **www.els.net/WileyCDA/ElsArticle/refld-a0021904.html**.

Lynn, Bill. "Incidental Take Permit Applications for Alabama Beach Mouse; Gulf Shores, Alabama." *Federal Register*, 24 May 2016, **www.federalregister.gov/documents/2016/05/24/2016-12159/incidental-take-permit-applications-for-alabama-beach-mouse-gulf-shores-alabama**.

"Daphne Ecological Services Field Office Frequently Asked
    Questions: Building Permits and the Alabama Beach
    Mouse." *U.S. Fish & Wildlife Service*, Mar. 2006,
    **www.fws.gov/daphne/es/abm/pdf/ABM-QA-HCP-3-
    17-06.pdf**.

Gabriel, Melissa Nelson. "Tiny Perdido Key Beach Mouse a
    Big Problem for Developers." *Pensacola News Journal*,
    Pensacola News Journal, 11 June 2016,

    **www.pnj.com/story/news/local/perdido-gulf-
shores/2016/06/11/tiny-perdido-key-beach-mouse-big-
problem-developers/85260034/**.

Wilder, Lundy. "Gulf State Park--Gulf Shores, Alabama
    Hurricane Ivan Damage." *Gulf Shores Alabama*, 20 July
    2016, **www.gulf-shores-alabama.net/gulf-state-park-
ivan-damage.html**.

Coffaro, Devan, and Ronald Gaines. "Details on $7 Million
Plan to Restore East End of Dauphin Island." *FOX10 News*, 6
Sept. 2015, **www.fox10tv.com/story/29968952/state-approves-
7-million-plan-to-restore-east-end-of-dauphin-island**.

Creamer, Jamie, and Katie Jackson. "Hurricane Opal Takes Its
    Toll on Beach Mouse Populations: Illustrates
    Importance of Deep Dune Systems on Gulf Coast
    Beaches." *A-Z Index | Map | People Finder Agricultural
    Communications and Marketing Alabama Agricultural
    Experiment Station and College of Agriculture*, 3 Jan. 1996,
    www.ag.auburn.edu/comm/news/1996/hurricane.php.

Swilling, William R., et al. "Population Dynamics of Alabama
        Beach Mice (PeromyscusPolionotusAmmobates)
        Following Hurricane Opal." *Biomedical Search - Medical
        Research and Health Resources*, 1 Oct. 1998,
        **www.biomedsearch.com/article/Population-
        dynamics-Alabama-beach-mice/53289268.html**.

US Department of Commerce, and NOAA. "Hurricane
        Frederic - September 12, 1979." *National Weather Service*,
        NOAA's National Weather Service, 21 Nov. 2016,
        www.weather.gov/mob/frederic.

"Hurricane Frederic." *Wikipedia*, Wikimedia Foundation, 19
        June 2018, **en.wikipedia.org/wiki/Hurricane_Frederic**.

Sloss, Craig R., et al. "Coastal Dunes: Geomorphology."
        Nature News, Nature Publishing Group, 2012,
        **www.nature.com/scitable/knowledge/library/coastal-
        dunes-geomorphology-25822000**.

"Bon Secour National Wildlife Refuge." *Wikipedia*, Wikimedia
Foundation, 19 June 2018,
en.wikipedia.org/wiki/BonSecourNationalWildlifeRefuge.

The Conservation Fund. "Coastal Protection at Bon Secour
        National Wildlife Refuge." *The Conservation Fund*, 13
        Feb. 2018, **www.conservationfund.org/news-
        resources/press-releases/1782-coastal-protection-at-
        bon-secour-national-wildlife-refuge**.

Dute, Jeff. "Last Large Parcel of Privately Held Alabama Relic
        Beach Habitat Focus of Preservation Effort." *AL.com*,
        AL.com, 4 Sept. 2013,
        **blog.al.com/live/2013/09/last_large_parcel_of_privatel
        y.html**.

Coffee, Glenn. "Corps Admits to Contributing to Erosion of Dauphin Island." *Sierra Club*, Sierra Club, 4 Mar. 2018, **www.sierraclub.org/alabama/blog/2018/03/corps-admits-contributing-erosion-dauphin-island**.

Wilder, Lundy. "Fort Morgan / Gulf Shores." *Fort Morgan Alabama Wildlife Photos*, 20 July 2016, **www.fort-morgan-condo.com/fort-morgan-wildlife.html**.

www.ingramcontent.com/pod-product-compliance
Lightning Source LLC
Chambersburg PA
CBHW031154250726

48655CB00002B/966